The Elusive Here & Now

Inspirational Poetry for the Soul

FIRST EDITION
First Printing, 2004

Photography by Dan Coppersmith
Cover Design by Denise Houseberg

Library of Congress Control Number: 2004115120
Coppersmith, Dan 1956—-
    The Elusive Here and Now: Inspirational Poetry for the Soul /
    Dan Coppersmith-1st ed.
    p.   cm.
    ISBN 0-97193406-1

An Out of This World® Production does not participate in, endorse, or have any authority or responsibility concerning private business transactions between our authors and the public.

All mail addressed to the author will be forwarded, but the publisher cannot, unless specifically instructed by the author, give out an address or phone number.

If you wish to contact the author or would like more information on this book, please write to the author in care of An Out of This World® Production and we will forward your request. Please write to:

Dan Coppersmith
c/o An Out of This World® Production
P.O. Box 610943
Dallas, TX 75261-0943

www.outofthisworldpublishing.com

ACKNOWLEDGMENTS

To the people behind Star's Edge International®. The Avatar® Course helped me grow in so many ways. It opened my mind and heart, and allowed me to create my life deliberately and joyfully. Many of the poems in this book were inspired by experiences connected with Avatar. I would like to express my gratitude to Harry, Avra, the Trainers, QMs, and the entire Avatar network for their love, support, and ongoing contribution to humanity.

To all who have supported me or my writing with encouragement, appreciation, or friendship. You have helped bring this book into being. The ripples continue. Thank you.

To Denise Houseberg, for helping me pull it all together. You are awesome!

Table of Contents

The Journey Home

Longing, searching
Struggling to find
Someplace inside
Called peace of mind

Hidden by doubt
Smothered by fear
Beneath such noise
I cannot hear

Wanting to feel
Yearning to see
Knowing there's more
Still inside me

What will I find
Behind the wall?
What's left of ME
Under it all?

Each step closer
Brightens the way
I must move on
I cannot stay

I've tasted life
As it could be
I will not rest
'Til I am free

Free from judgment
And free to feel
With open heart
Be me; be real

Beliefs set free
Give back to me
Power to choose
Freedom to be.

Change the World

Blessings come in many ways
Bright sunshine and rainy days
Sweet success and failure too —
Depends upon your point of view

Judgments fall in many shades
A pretty girl, a man with AIDS
This is good, that is bad
Based upon a belief you had

Realities, seen as true
Are filtered through a point of view
Widen back, free your mind
Oh, the choices you will find!

Be flexible in your point of view
Try out many, keep a few
As your beliefs are allowed to change
So your world will rearrange.

Just Like Me

I'm the only one I know
Who's wanting to belong
The only one who's said "Why me?"
While trying to be strong

I'm the only one who gets confused
And thinks they must pretend
For fear of someone finding out
They didn't comprehend

I'm the only one desiring
To be loved for who they are
The only one who's felt betrayed
Still dealing with the scar

I'm the only one who's felt left out
Just wanting to be accepted
The only one afraid to ask
For fear of being rejected

I'm the only one who's been depressed
And thought nobody cared
The only one needing to move on
But still just too darn scared

I'm the only one who feels remorse
For something that they did
The only one, for fear of shame
Who keeps their secrets hid

I'm the only one who's been hurt before
The only one needing a friend
The only one wanting to open up
But still feeling the need to defend

If only I wasn't the only one
If there were others just like me
The separation would dissolve
If it wasn't about just me.

Believing is Seeing

Though your eyes and mine
Work the same way
More than just vision
Comes into play

The viewpoints we take
The judgments we hold
Greatly determine
How life will unfold

Beliefs we hold dear
Be they helpful or not
Attract what is needed
To fill in the plot

Bending and shifting
What you perceive
Your world will conform
To what you believe.

Renaissance Man

How it all started
I do not recall
Before it was over
My kingdom would fall

The castle was built
With hard work and long hours
Impregnable walls
Concealing a coward

Royal denial
Of injustice done
Kept me from trusting
Anyone

Protected by armor
Too heavy to play
Cold and alone
Consuming my day

The moat kept full
The drawbridge closed
In control
Detached and composed

Locked in the dungeon
Too dark to reveal
Secrets kept hidden
Unable to feel

The foundation tested
It all fell apart
Chains unraveled
Revealing my heart

Dying and bleeding
Trembling and reeling
Kicking and screaming
Crying and feeling

Exploring the ruins
The identity lost
Amazed at the lesson
Amazed at the cost

Strength, my weakness
Honesty, my salvation
I stand here naked
In awe of my creation.

Just One Day

The fog lifted
To clear blue sky
A sea of choices
Floating by

The scent of ferns
On a gentle breeze
Conveying a message
Of peace and ease

Water trickling
Through moss covered rocks
Graciously allowing
The soul to detox

Trees stretching to light
With unquestioned resolve
Tranquil and calm
Troubles dissolve

New life springing
From death and decay
Leaving behind
Fear and dismay

Shadows changing
As Earth revolves
Viewpoints shift
The spirit evolves

Butterflies lullabied
By crickets' song
Aware in the moment
No right, no wrong

The mist settled in
Quieting the abyss
In gratitude
For a day such as this.

Miracles

Butterflies that flit about
Laughter from a child's mouth
Birds hanging in the breeze
Tell me, do you think of these?

Sunsets shared on the beach
The glory of a mountain peak
The magic in a flake of snow
Are these places that you go?

Lost in clouds made of cotton
Friends far away, but not forgotten
Raindrops falling on your face
Are these allowed in your space?

The pleasure in a gentle touch
Flowers and trees and stars and such
Secret places that you find
Miracles are in your mind.

Eternal

We came here, it seems
To grow and evolve
With lessons to learn
And things to resolve

What purpose we have
Is not always clear
Sometimes we struggle
With doubt and fear

Each on our own path
Each at our own pace
Yet all are connected
Through trials and grace

This life is a journey
And though it must end
Continuing onward
Spirits transcend.

Evolution

It's raining out there
Clouds fill the sky
I'm struggling in here
Wondering why

Why did she leave?
Will she ever come home?
Why do I feel
So lost and alone?

Why is my heart
Filled with such pain?
How can the clouds
Hold so much rain?

Inside and outside
The storm so intense
Why doesn't my life
Make any sense?

From the darkness that wishes
The storm would subside
Came a flash of brilliance
My eyes opened wide

The insight that came
From beyond comprehension
All of this pain
Just to get my attention

Teardrops and raindrops
Washed away the facade
I could see clearly
My beliefs were flawed

These beliefs-
What I'd based my life upon
Had been running things
For way too long

Where did they come from?
What makes them so?
These were things
I wanted to know

And so I explored
The beliefs I'd been holding
And how they affected
The life they'd been molding

Some came from anger
Defiance or shame
Some of them served me
Some were quite lame

Some came from parents
Back when I was young
Some gave no clue
From where they had come

Some came from church
Some came from school
One group or another
Imposing their rule

Many beliefs
No longer made sense
And were carried around
At great expense

In letting them go
New life has come
Dark clouds have lifted
Unveiling the sun

With judgments returning
To neutral ground
Limitless choices
Appear all around

This redefinition
Has opened my mind
And opened new worlds
To which I'd been blind

A path has been cleared
To an inner knowing
That guides and directs
As I'm learning and growing

The storm of emotions
The clouds of gray
Helped bring me
Where I am today

And though that union
Has come to an end
I'm proud to call
The woman my friend.

Knowtions

How our life
Turns out to be
Should not be deemed
A mystery

The epic saga
Will unfold
According to
The beliefs we hold

Merely accepting
A belief as true
Invests attention
In that view

After which
The world will show
What it is
We think we know

On this proof
The ego grows
Inflated by
This thing it knows

As it grows
Our minds close
And we see only
What we chose

Other views
No matter how pristine
Remain obscure
And can't be seen

We can't change
And we can't grow
'Till we look beyond
What we know

Our beliefs are reflected
In the world outside
Let your life
Be your guide

Question all
You take for granted
We only harvest
What's been planted.

Snow

Gentle flakes
Soft and white
Drifting, falling
Through the night

In silent wonder
As I slept
Glistening secrets
Darkness kept

With morning light
Appearing bright
Peering out
Brought pure delight

The mundane world
I thought I knew
Had been transformed
To something new

The filters
I'd been seeing with
Could not survive
This viewpoint shift

It shocked me into
Present time
Beyond the trappings
Of my mind

Here and now
In awe and wonder
Dissolving illusions
I'd been under

Nature's beauty
So intensely real
Hearts spill open
And people feel

In this space
We come alive
In this joy
Our spirits thrive

Seek the beauty
In all things
Feel gratitude
At what life brings

Stop and smell the roses
Breathe the sparkling air
The magic in that flake of snow
Is lurking everywhere.

You Decide

As a child we're so free, so full of life
With character and heart to spare
In our natural state, we play and create
Live and love with never a care

As we grow and learn, we take on beliefs
As simply as breathing the air
This, over time, closes our minds
And what's worse, we're not even aware

Now that we've grown into proper adults
Full of limits and filters galore
Our attention isn't free, as it once used to be
Our vision isn't clear anymore

We each view the world through filters, you see
Our beliefs, the glasses we're using
This we have done since we were young
With so many, life can be confusing

Often, we don't even know they are there
Beliefs can be quite transparent
Affecting each glance, each circumstance
Just how, not always apparent

It's up to us to clean the lens
To remove the obstructions from view
Open our eyes, prepare for surprise
Instead of just what's assumed true

We all have the power to believe what we want
We all are quite able to choose
Deliberately create, determine our fate
Travel down new avenues

Fact is, we still can be anything …
The limits we know came from where?
Let them all go, as you stretch and grow
Create the life you want, if you dare.

Flaming White Horse

Words take form
Beneath my pen
Reflecting places
I have been

Adventures taken
Lessons learned
Choices made
Wisdom earned

Memories drifting
In my mind
Remnants of
Another time

Times I've struggled
And made it through
Old beliefs
Displaced by new

Relationships
That didn't last
Stuck attention
In the past

The turbulence
Of changing years
Forced to face
Relentless fears

As members of
The human race
We all have demons
We must face

Love and loss
Dragons slain
We've all known joy
We've all felt pain

It seems we're after
Similar things
Searching for peace
Spreading our wings

Releasing the crap
It took years to acquire
Climbing our way
Back out of the mire

A prince to come save us
On his flaming white horse
Who'll get the steed
Should it end in divorce?

For our hearts to be happy
And our minds to be still
Consider how sacred
The gift of free will.

Cohle Grace

We each have a mission
A reason we're here
Stretching and growing
Finding love in fear

Or perhaps we came
To bring light to the Earth
And the world's been changed
Because of our birth

One such being
Was named Cohle Grace
Her healing presence
Still ripples through space

Her time here was short
Her visit was brief
Her birth was filled
With wonder and grief

Though the shell that housed
Her essence is gone
She remains with us
Her beacon shines on

In celebrating
Her life and her death
The joy she brought
Without breathing a breath

With love and support
With family and friend
We honor her spirit
And her choice to ascend

We may never know
Why she chose to leave
Yet our lives are affected
By what we believe

Perhaps her intention
Before returning above
Was simply to experience
Unconditional love.

Once Upon A Time

Long, long ago
And not so very far away
A world was created
Where spirits could play

The rules were very simple
First create and then explore
Experience it fully
Then go create some more

But somewhere in this game of life
Judgment entered in
Resisting our creations
Became the mortal sin

With resistance and denial
Came the fall of man
Suffering was introduced
Into the master plan

His energy consumed
Sustaining this resistance
The world filled with tired souls
Resisting their existence

Entrenched in denial
Convinced his hell is real
Justified and rationalized
In think instead of feel

Until we can experience
The things that we resist
Until we can appreciate
Peace will not exist

Judgment must be given up
With compassion, we must feel
Embrace all facets of ourselves
Allow our world to heal.

In Us All

In a world full of wonder
In a sleep full of dreams
In a heart full of laughter
In us all, it would seem

In the awe of a rainbow
In the clouds floating by
In soft ocean breezes
In us all, you and I

In the song of a sparrow
As it welcomes the sun
In the mist of the morning
In us all, every one

In the Earth beneath us
In the heavens above
At the core of our being
In us all, there is love.

The Continuing Saga

A radiant spirit
Who loved to explore
In search of adventure
Human, once more.

Only You

No one on Earth
Exists quite like you
And no one is able
To do what you do

The person you are
The talents you bear
Gifts that only
You can share

Only you have learned
From the things you've done
Gaining perspective
From the battles you've won

Times when you've lost
Have been priceless too
The lessons contribute
To what makes you you

The rest of the world
Can't see through your eyes
Which is why your insight
May be such a prize

Because you are you
There are lives you affect
Much more than you
Would ever expect

The things you do
The things you say
Send ripples throughout
The Milky Way

You're unique, amazing
Like no one else
You have the exclusive
On being yourself.

Food For Thought

Sometimes we whine
Gripe and complain
Singing the victim's
Familiar refrain

Blaming the world
For all that's wrong
Each new day
The same old song

It's a trap we crawl into
A place where we hide
Keeping our spirit
Stuffed deep inside

Somehow forgetting
We determine our fate
That the life which we lead
We chose to create

Each decision we make
Each thought we embrace
Affects the complexion
Of the world we face

If our food for thought
Is a negative meal
That is what
We will taste as real

If we dwell on anger
Injustice and pain
We'll tend to attract
More of the same

If we suffer, hopeless
At the mercy of all
We are the ones
Keeping us small

Placing the blame
On somebody else
Puts the solution
Outside of ourselves

Recognizing
We are Source
Awakens the captain
To master his course.

Lessons From Nature

Imagine…

A stream in the woods
With no one around
Where the babbling of nature
Is the only sound

Listen intently
To what you will hear
Relax for a moment
The message is clear

Surrender yourself
To the song of the stream
Let the life giving water
Sweep you into a dream

Learn from the water
To dance and to sing
And not to be troubled
By any old thing

See how the current
Flows over and around
No matter the obstacle
You'll not see a frown

It doesn't get mad
If you stand in its way
It welcomes the chance
To splash and to play

It nurtures all life
Be it fish, plant or tree
It offers a drink
On its way to the sea

The stream offers lessons
So simple; no fuss
Imagine the ripples
If applied to us.

A Reminder

I am enough
Just me alone
With no one's approval
Only my own

I am complete
With no need for more
Containing within me
An infinite store

I am abundance
I am magic and light
I am creation
I am joy and delight

I am Source of it all
I am boundless, and yet
Being still human
Sometimes I forget.

Yellow

You think it's just a color
But it's vibrant and alive
It sings to the world, "Look at me — I will hide no more!"

You think it's just a color
But it's bold and exciting
It screams, "Come play with me! Feel my energy!"

You think it's just a color
But it's sunshine and laughter
It's the brilliant celebration of life in bloom!

You think it's just a color
You try to ignore it, but you can't
Because it calls to you
It shouts from the rooftops, "WAKE UP!!!"

You think it's just a color

You think I'm just a man.

Imagine No Limits

Such a glorious morning
Glistening with dew
Sun climbing gently
Sky full of blue

A day to be treasured
A world to explore
Imagine no limits
Just that, nothing more

Each day starts
With a clean slate
It's all up to you
What will you create?

Will you kindle the dreams
Left dormant inside
Igniting the passion
On which you thrive?

Will you honor
The mighty creator in you
With something exciting
And new to pursue?

When faced with things
That could annoy
Will you choose instead
To find the joy?

Will you live in the moment
Or dwell in the past?
Will this day be brand new
Or just like the last?

Each sunrise
Brings a new chance
To make new choices
To let your soul dance

Such a glorious morning
Sky full of blue
Imagine no limits
What will you do?